Preface

The invasion of exotic species has always been an intriguing and important ecological topic. With the advent of modern molecular techniques that enable the transfer of genes from one organism to another, whether or not they are closely related, we have a new class of 'exotic' organisms which may escape or be released into the environment. What will be the consequences of such new invasions? Will they be more or less damaging than the more traditional foreign exotics? The purpose of this fourth Ecological Issues Booklet is to address some of these questions.

The contributors (page 46) met for two days, in April 1992, at Losehill Hall Field Centre in Derbyshire, to write a draft manuscript of the booklet, which we subsequently refined in Leeds. The first pair of chapters introduce the reader to the two fundamental areas, one molecular and one ecological, that form the background to the subject. The next three chapters concentrate on the knowledge available for, and problems associated with, different classes of organisms. However, because both of these are different for microorganisms, plants and animals, these three chapters do not have a common format.

We are extremely grateful to all the contributors who helped us to edit the booklet by reading various drafts. We would also like to thank Andrew Davis, Lynne O'Brien and Sheena McNamee who made helpful comments on the final manuscript.

Bryan Shorrocks and David Coates
Leeds, January 1993

THE RELEASE OF GENETICALLY ENGINEERED ORGANISMS

CONTENTS

1. INTRODUCTION TO GENETIC ENGINEERING

This chapter gives a brief description of Genetically Modified Organisms (GMOs) and the techniques involved in producing them.

1.1 What is a GMO?

Part VI (para. 4) of the Environmental Protection Act (1990) gives the following definition:

"For the purposes of this Part an organism is 'genetically modified' if any of the genes or other genetic material in the organism-

(a) have been modified by means of an artificial technique prescribed in regulations by the Secretary of State; or

(b) are inherited or otherwise derived, through any number of replications, from genes or other genetic material (from any source) which were so modified."

These "artificial techniques" involve ways of creating new combinations of genetic material which cannot be achieved by traditional breeding or other natural methods. They include the use of **recombinant DNA** technology (see below) and artificial cell fusion or hybridization, including protoplast fusion (largely restricted to plants). A **transgenic** organism or **GMO** is one which carries introduced recombinant DNA in its genome.

Many GMOs will carry only one extra gene. In some cases this gene may originate from the same species, possibly with some modification from the native version. Such GMOs might be thought of as simply new variants or strains, particularly in the light of the levels of genetic variation existing naturally in most species. In others, the additional gene will be wholly or partly derived from other species, possibly very distantly related, and may thus confer novel properties on the GMO. Some GMOs, such as those arising from cell fusion or hybridization, can be considered as new species.

1.2 Genes and gene expression

The framework within which biological diversity operates is now conceptually very clear, based on a common system of information storage. The details of how this information is converted to a useful product, usually a protein, do not concern us here (for a good explanation, see Murrell & Roberts, 1989), but it should be emphasised that the system is both chemically and functionally the same in all living organisms. At the molecular level, all organisms are much more similar than might be imagined by looking at them. The phenotypic differences we see are often the result of altered patterns of gene expression, not different combinations of genes.

Information is stored in the nucleic acids found within all living organisms, either deoxyribonucleic acid (DNA), or ribonucleic acid (RNA) in the case of many viruses. The information required for normal growth and development of the cell, and hence of the organism, is written as a linear code using a four letter 'alphabet'. The correct expression of this information leads to much of the diversity we see, by producing particular proteins in varying amounts at different stages of development, and in different parts of the organism. This regulation of gene expression is also a function of the DNA sequence, and is often controlled by stretches of DNA called **promoters**, found adjacent to the **coding regions**.

Expression of a gene occurs when the information held in the DNA is used to direct the synthesis of (usually) a protein. In the first step in the process, **transcription**, the DNA code is copied to form messenger RNA (mRNA). The copying process starts at a site adjacent to the coding region, the promoter. In the second step the mRNA is **translated** into protein. Whether a coding region is transcribed or not depends on factors which affect the promoter and sequences around it. Regulation at the transcriptional level occurs at this stage, such that some promoter regions allow transcription to occur all the time, others only at certain times in development, or when specific conditions apply *e.g.* the heat shock proteins mentioned in Chapter 5.

In practice, the two components of the gene can be treated as separate entities: the coding sequence defines which protein is produced, the promoter and regulatory regions when and how much of it.

Other factors can affect gene expression, such as the physical structure of the chromosome around the gene. Regulation of gene expression does not only occur by directly regulating the amount of transcription. Large stretches of DNA can be inactivated by dense packaging of the **chromatin**; this is best seen during cell division, when the DNA is highly compacted to form the chromosomes, and when transcription is completely stopped. In this way, the local conformation of the chromosome can control the transcription of a gene, preventing or reducing expression. Under normal circumstances, these factors act together with the normal regulatory mechanisms.

The different chromosomal conformations are relevant to the introduction of new DNA sequences. The effect that the site of insertion has on the expression of the foreign DNA can be unpredictable, as certain structural conformations of the chromosome may impose a pattern of expression of the new gene. These so-called **position effects** mean that, in many cases, it is not possible fully to predict the level of expression, or indeed when in development the inserted DNA is expressed.

The other potential problem with inserting new DNA sequences into a genome is that of insertion within a coding region or regulatory region, leading to the disruption of the normal cellular processes. In fact, this appears to be highly unlikely in **eukaryotes**, as one feature of their genomes is the large amount of DNA which does not code for proteins. The function of most of this DNA is unknown; the consequence is that random integration of foreign DNA is usually into such regions, with no disruption of the normal complement of genes.

These problems only apply to the immediate products of gene manipulation in the laboratory. Strains and varieties produced for release and other purposes are selected to be stable constructs with known expression patterns.

1.3 Cloning and manipulation of DNA
A detailed explanation of these techniques can be found in Murrell & Roberts (1989), and Old & Primrose (1989).

Before an organism can be modified, the appropriate fragment(s) of DNA need to be isolated in large amounts from the source organism. This is the process of **DNA cloning**. Initially, DNA fragments are produced using **restriction enzymes** (which cut DNA at specific recognition sequences) or by the process of **cDNA** synthesis (creating a DNA copy of the messenger RNA molecule for the target gene).

These fragments are then inserted into a **cloning vector**, which allows each fragment produced to be purified. The most common cloning vectors are **plasmids**, extrachromosomal circular DNA molecules found in many bacteria, which are capable of replication independently of the bacterial chromosome. Insertion of the DNA fragment(s) into such a vector, introduction into a host bacterial cell and **amplification** of the recombinant vector will give rise to very large numbers of copies of the DNA fragments.

Usually DNA cloning results in a **library**, a complex mixture of different fragments. These are screened, using a variety of methods, to find the desired clone(s). Subsequent sequencing of the DNA in the purified clone will enable identification of promoters, coding sequences, etc.

Sometimes a cloned gene may be transferred directly into a target cell or organism; however, further manipulation of genes is commonly required. The most common such manipulation is the creation of a fusion gene, where the promoter from one gene is linked to the protein-encoding sequences from another gene, enabling alteration in the expression pattern of the protein (for an example of this, see Chapter 5).

Transferring DNA into cells, a process called **transformation**, and the subsequent integration of the foreign DNA into the host genome, are two separate events, each of which can be done using one of two basic approaches. Physical approaches to DNA transformation all depend on disrupting the cell membrane, or cell wall and membrane, to allow access to the cytoplasm. Methods include the use of heat shock or electric shock to disrupt membranes, microinjection and projectile bombardment to introduce the DNA into the cell through holes in the cell surface. Biological approaches, such as using viruses or the DNA transfer system used by some *Agrobacterium* species when they infect plants, subvert natural systems to introduce the new DNA sequences.

In **prokaryotes**, recombinant DNA is usually introduced in a plasmid or other vector and integration into the bacterial chromosome does not normally take place. In most eukaryotes, integration is required for the stable inheritance and expression of introduced sequences. Integration depends either on random or, more recently, homologous recombination. In some natural systems integration of DNA into the genome is a normal part of the life cycle, such as bacterial prophage production, retroviral integration, transposition (see later), or the *Agrobacterium* system. Integration by recombination produces new sequences that are stable; there is no reason why these new sequences should be any less stable than the rest of the DNA in the genome. The biological integrative forms have their own problems, the most extreme of which are found when using **transposable elements** as vectors.

Transposable elements are DNA sequences which have the ability to move around the genome. This movement depends on two characteristics: (1) specific sequences at each end of the transposable element which are required for insertion into and excision from the genomic DNA; and (2) a 'transposase' enzyme, usually encoded by the transposable element. Integration of foreign DNA sequences can be achieved by inserting the sequences into transposable elements *in vitro*, and microinjecting the new construct into cells, along with DNA coding for the transposase activity. The ability of transposable elements to move, albeit at low frequency, implies that sequences introduced using these as vectors may be less stable than those introduced by recombination, especially if the new gene is moved into a genetic background which includes active transposable elements. Movement of the introduced sequences may then have consequences resulting from the position effects discussed above, although these effects are in essence no different from the results of transposition within the non-modified host species.

1.4 Summary
All organisms use the same methods for passing on, using and storing the information required for their growth and development. Genetic

manipulation has given us the ability to move this information both within and between species, using methods adapted from, but not new to, natural processes. The introduced DNA sequences generally behave in exactly the same manner as the normal genes within the host organism.

2. INVASIONS

2.1 Are GMOs fundamentally different?

Animals and plants have been genetically modified by selective breeding for thousands of years. Genetic manipulation using recombinant DNA may only represent the latest and most powerful technique for the alteration of organisms (discussed by Levin 1989, 1990). It could, therefore, be argued that most proposed GMOs will fall into the same category as these traditional agricultural varieties, and pose little new risk to the environment. Alternatively, some GMOs may have sufficiently different phenotypes that they can not be regarded as varieties of native species, but rather as **exotics**. Among this group of plants and animals, which have been introduced to areas outside their normal range, there are numerous examples of organisms which have become major environmental problems.

2.2 Using invasions as a model for GMO release

An analysis of invasions by natural processes and deliberate releases will help to provide some measure of the risk of invasion by a transgenic organism, as there is no *a priori* reason to suppose that a GMO should behave any differently to any other introduced species. This analogy of transgenics with novel invaders is far from perfect, as most modifications would be relatively minor and well understood changes to the genome of a native species. Most ecological invasions are by totally exotic genotypes, often freed from their competitors, predators and pathogens that keep them in check in their native habitats. Therefore, it would be fair to suggest that the analysis of natural invasions greatly overestimates the risk of invasions by GMOs. If an organism that was both transgenic and exotic were to be released, the risks associated with invasion would be due to its exotic rather than its transgenic nature.

The release of GMOs, both deliberate and accidental, poses two potential classes of problem:

i. The spread of the foreign gene to other species by horizontal transfer (see following chapters). This could lead to the creation of novel transgenics with new properties.

ii. The GMO behaves in a similar way to an invasive species. This is equivalent to a natural invasion.

2.3 What is an invasion?

An invasion can be defined simply as the introduction or release of an organism into a region where it was not formerly native. Exotic species have been deliberately released for a wide variety of reasons ranging from ornamental plants to insect biological control agents. Elton (1958), in his book *The Ecology of Invasions*, described an invasion as 'an ecological explosion' which implies that they are bound to create an environmental problem of some kind. Most introductions of exotic species however, both deliberate and accidental, fail completely and many that do establish are not an ecological problem. There are four stages through which invaders have to pass before they become a pest. Invaders start with a propagule (founder group) (1); which may then become established as a local colony (2); and may then become a naturalised widespread exotic (3); finally becoming a pest or weed (4).

2.4 Estimating the risk of natural invasions

Two estimates of the probability of a successful introduction and subsequent pest have been made, both using large data sets covering very large numbers of releases and invasions:

i. Williamson & Brown (1986) examined recorded natural and deliberate invasions into the UK in the last 100 years. They concluded that:
   - about 10% of invaders become established.
   - about 10% of those go on to become pests.
   - therefore an introduced species has about a 1% chance of becoming a pest.

   Using data on angiosperms in the UK, Williamson (1993) determined that 12.8% of 1642 species of introduced plants have become established and 6.7% of those established have become severe pests (0.85% of the total).

ii. Groves (1986), using data on plant introductions in Australia, estimated that 4-6 species are becoming established each year. Groves estimated:
   - about 10% of introduced species become established.
   - about 1-2% of introduced species become weeds.

These data sets have been drawn from different parts of the world but provide very similar estimates of the success of plant introductions.

2.5 Some natural invasions in Britain

(1) *Rhododendron ponticum* is native to the area around the Black Sea and was first introduced into Britain by plant collectors. Its subsequent use as an ornamental plant, and cover species for game birds, led to its widespread planting throughout the country and subsequent invasion into woodland and heathland. Many might regard the plant as a colourful addition to our flora although it does have a major ecological effect on the native trees. *Rhododendron* forms such a dense canopy that ground cover plants, including the saplings of trees, are almost totally excluded. Thus the succession process is disturbed and as trees die they are not replaced, creating stands of pure exotics.

(2) *Spartina anglica* is a salt marsh grass formed by natural hybridization between a native species, *S. maritima*, and an accidentally introduced exotic, *S. alterniflora*. Neither of the parent species is particularly invasive. Indeed both are declining in Britain, whereas their hybrid is an extremely aggressive colonizer that has spread to cover 10000 ha of British salt marshes in the century since the appearance of the hybrid (Gray *et al.*, 1991).

(3) Dutch Elm Disease is caused by a pathogenic fungus carried by a beetle which attacks Elms (*Ulmus* spp). In a very few years the disease devastated British elms and transformed many landscapes. Elms were the predominant woody species in many hedgerows which have now been lost as a result. There is no evidence that any species has been made extinct in Britain as a result of the disease, although there have been declines in many species of birds such as the chaffinch (*Fringilla coelebs*), which requires high song-posts, chiffchaff (*Phylloscopus collybita*) and goldcrest (*Regulus regulus*), which feed on elms, and jackdaw (*Corvus monedula*) and barn owl (*Tyto alba*), which require high, safe tree-holes for nesting. Conversely, there were temporary increases in invertebrates feeding on decaying wood and the woodpeckers and nuthatches which feed on them.

2.6 Environmental effects of invaders

The effects of introduced mammals and birds have been quite well documented throughout the world. A huge literature review of such introductions (Ebenhard, 1988; summarised on pp.22-23 in the Royal Commission on Environmental Pollution, 1989) using over 400 papers, describing over 1500 events, identified six principal categories of ecological effects.

   i.   Damage to plants or habitat.
   ii.   Imbalance in prey caused by predation.
   iii.   Competition for resources.
   iv.   Spread of parasites/disease.
   v.   Breeding with indigenous species to produce hybrids.
   vi.   Becoming an additional source of prey for indigenous species.

The probabilities calculated by Ebenhard (1988) of different types of damage occurring are tabulated below.

Effect	Birds %	Mammals %
Plant / Habitat damage	20	0
Significant impact on native species by predation	17	1
Significant impact on native species by competition	3	4
TOTAL	40	5

These broad ecological effects will apply just as well to other animals and, to a lesser extent, plants and microorganisms. However, it is clear that, as there is such a difference between mammals and birds, predictions about the likelihood of each outcome in different groups might not be appropriate.

2.7 Why do some invaders establish?
Identification of habitat types which might be the most vulnerable to invasion provides additional data for the calculation of the probability that an organism may become a problem. Crawley (1986, 1987) has shown that, in Britain, a disproportionate number of exotic plants are found in early successional or disturbed habitats. In the most severe case 78% of plants found in urban wasteland are exotics, whereas on

mountain summits this falls to 0%, with other habitats having intermediate values. The best indicator of the invasibility of a particular habitat is the degree of ground cover, with habitats of low cover having a higher proportion of exotic species.

In order to understand what kinds of organisms may be successful invaders, Williamson & Brown (1986) listed some suggested characteristics of invasive species:

> from distant areas
> climatically matched
> r-selected (high birth rates and/or low mortality)
> high dispersal
> low competition with indigenous species
> lack of natural enemies
> inbreeding
> single-parent reproduction
> finding an empty niche

These characteristics were only intended as rules of thumb and there are examples of species which have become successful invaders with none of these characteristics (Perrins *et al.*, 1992). In fact, Gray (1986) found that invasive plants in Britain have no particular genetic characteristics in common.

Lawton & Brown (1986) could not make any firm prediction of the success of any particular species introduction, although those species which tended to have lower fluctuations in species numbers were more likely to persist. They also found that when comparing all animals introduced to the British Isles, the chance of successful establishment was positively correlated with body size whereas when considering only insects the relationship was reversed.

2.8 Are all colonizers pests?

Once established, only a small proportion of colonizers become pests or weeds and adversely affect their new environment. Simberloff (1981, 1991) found no clear demonstration of any effect on the community or ecosystem in 79.4% of cases, and suggested that successful invaders were merely occupying vacant niches in established communities. This hypothesis was severely criticised by Herbold & Moyle (1986), who found that most invasions had a clear demonstrable effect on the numbers of species in a community.

In an attempt to identify the common features of pest plants, Baker (1965) listed 14 characteristics of an ideal weed which described a plastic, super-generalist with immense powers of reproduction and dispersal. No single species possesses all Baker's features and possession of any will not necessarily make the species a weed. Newsome & Noble (1986) found only limited support for the presence of Baker's weedy characters in the exotics of the Australian flora. In contrast they found that successful invaders were specialists often occupying a very restricted habitat range.

2.9 Summary

The body of literature on invasions is about the accidental or deliberate release of exotic species, as these are the organisms which have produced problems in the past. Although this provides some insight into the possible fate of released GMOs, the model is only applicable to an extent. Perhaps a more appropriate model is the release of novel genotypes of native species (about which there is very little information), or the introduction of new strains of plants already in cultivation, and which have caused no problems. It must be stressed that ecological problems arising from the introduction of organisms which are both exotic and transgenic may be largely the result of the exotic rather than transgenic nature of the organism. Care must be taken to assess the potential risks of release on a case by case basis. Problems to be addressed will be different in microbes, plants and animals, and they are discussed individually in the following three chapters.

3. RELEASE OF MICROORGANISMS

3.1 Introduction

There have already been many trial releases of genetically manipulated bacteria and viruses, aimed at eventual applications such as the control of crop pests and diseases or enhanced plant growth. Genetically manipulated fungi will also become available for these purposes, and other uses expected in future include the cleaning up of effluents and environmental pollution, and the extraction of minerals. In many cases, non-GMOs are already in use without any recorded adverse environmental consequences and the proposed GMOs represent relatively small improvements over existing practice. Despite this history of successful use, our knowledge of ecology and population genetics is still much more rudimentary for microbes than for higher organisms. However, rapid progress is now being aided by the techniques of molecular genetics and stimulated by the interest in GMOs. Our ability to describe the effect of an introduction on the indigenous microbial community, even after the event, is still very limited, so any predictive assessment must rely more on empirical experience than on an understanding of the community structure. In the long term, however, public acceptance of the many potential benefits of the introduction of genetically modified microorganisms will be hard to gain unless ecologists can demonstrate a clearer understanding of natural microbial communities.

3.2 Microbial communities

Nutrient recycling in the environment is mediated by complex communities of microorganisms. Aquatic habitats tend towards a more homogeneous distribution of the microflora, but microbial activity in the soil is localised by the uneven distribution of nutrient sources. The status of microbial populations in the environment is always difficult to judge. Many individuals will be dormant as spores or cysts and there is evidence that those bacteria incapable of forming such structures can enter a viable but non-culturable state. This, together with the existence of many species yet to be cultivated *in vitro*, accounts for the enormous discrepancy between direct microscopic and viable counts, for bacteria at least. Thus, it is against this background of heterogeneous and poorly

Conjugation

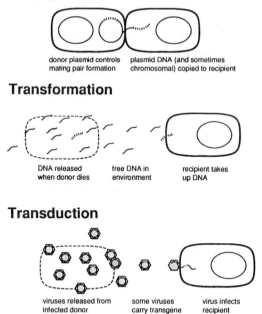

donor plasmid controls   plasmid DNA (and sometimes
mating pair formation   chromosomal) copied to recipient

Transformation

DNA released   free DNA in   recipient takes
when donor dies   environment   up DNA

Transduction

viruses released from   some viruses   virus infects
infected donor   carry transgene   recipient

Fig. 3.1. The three main processes that could lead to transfer of introduced DNA between bacteria.

Each of these processes is widespread, but not universal. **Conjugation** involves physical contact between donor and recipient cells, and depends on a set of transfer genes in the donor cell. Normally these transfer genes are carried on a plasmid (plasmids are present as a natural component of most bacterial genomes), and their main function is probably to ensure the transfer of the plasmid that carries them, but in the conjugation process other plasmids, and sometimes chromosomal DNA, may also be transferred. Transfer of bacterial DNA by phages (viruses that attack bacteria) is called **transduction**; fragments of host DNA may be erroneously packaged into phage particles (generalized transduction), or phages that integrate into the genome may take some of the adjacent DNA when they excise (specialized transduction). **Transformation** occurs when bacteria take up naked DNA from the environment - some will only admit DNA from their own species, but others can acquire totally foreign DNA.

defined populations that the question of gene transfer is to be addressed. The colonisation of dead organic material, or the formation of biofilms on, for example, root and leaf surfaces, provides the spatial arrangement necessary for gene transfer. In habitats rich in nutrients, *e.g.* composts, the active state of the microflora would also tend to promote the possibility of gene exchange. The fate of an exotic microorganism introduced into such a community from whatever source can be difficult to determine. For example, "die-back", where the population declines below the limit of detection but remains viable and capable of proliferation, is indistinguishable from "die-out", where the organism does not survive. The practice of environmental microbiology is always constrained by such limitations. When a GMO is involved, there is the additional question of whether the introduced genetic material has survived or been transferred, irrespective of the fate of the host.

3.3 Gene survival and transfer

On the basis of laboratory studies, three main mechanisms for bacterial gene transfer have been defined: conjugation, transduction and transformation (Fig. 3.1).

Gene transfer in bacteria is not necessarily restricted to donors and recipients that are closely related, although the majority of successful transfers are between close relatives, because the incoming DNA is more likely to function and is more readily stabilized by homologous recombination. A striking illustration of the effectiveness of wide-range genetic transfer is the spread of antibiotic resistance among bacteria of medical importance, in response to the very strong selective pressures imposed by the clinical use of antibiotics. Many different species have acquired the same resistance genes; in most cases these genes are within transposable elements on wide host-range plasmids, which explains their great mobility. This example shows that natural mechanisms for the spread of genes are undoubtedly present in bacteria, but also that the eventual fate of genes depends primarily on the selective forces that favour their survival. Two approaches have confirmed that gene transfer occurs in bacterial species that are potential candidates for GMO release. The distribution of natural genetic variation shows that plasmids move between strains with different chromosomal backgrounds in field populations of *Rhizobium* (Young & Wexler, 1988). This approach can detect processes that may take many years to become apparent, whereas the more direct approach of introducing a marked strain and looking for recombinants is inevitably limited in duration. Indeed, when a genetically modified variant of the same *Rhizobium* species was introduced into field populations, no transfer of the marker could be detected, even though it was carried on a transmissible plasmid (Hirsch & Spokes, 1988). Marker transfer has, however, been detected in a number of studies of other bacteria in microcosms or quasi-natural environments (see papers in the book edited by Fry & Day, 1988). Conjugation has been most often studied, but there is evidence that transformation and transduction also occur at significant frequencies in bacterial populations (see Stotzky & Babich, 1986).

In order to reduce the possibility of genetic transfer as far as possible, the introduced DNA should be located in the chromosome rather than on a plasmid or in an active transposable element, and the strain should not carry plasmids or phages that might confer donor ability. Once released, however, the GMO might receive such ability from indigenous bacteria, so such "genetic containment" cannot be regarded as absolute.

3.4 Deliberate release compared with contained use
Recombinant bacteria are already used to produce a range of medical products such as human growth hormone and insulin. These recombinants are designed so that their survival in the environment is practically impossible (biological containment). For the deliberate release of a GMO, a degree of persistence is essential and this is reflected in the design of the genetic construct. Balancing this against the desire to limit gene transfer to the indigenous population is difficult, and in any case the possibility of transfer can never be excluded. The favoured approach is to consider only the release of genes whose potential dissemination in the resident microflora would clearly give no grounds for concern.

3.5 Alternatives to the use of GMOs
It is important that the development of a specific GMO is not perceived as the automatic biological response to a particular agricultural application or environmental problem. For pollution incidents, treatment

of the contaminated environment by promoting the growth of indigenous biodegradative microbes has been used to good effect. The quite dramatic success of nutrient supplementation in the recovery of beaches contaminated in the Exxon Valdez oil spill is an excellent example (see Prince, 1992). Release of unmodified microorganisms or their products can also be considered before resorting to GMOs. *Bacillus thuringiensis* insecticidal toxins have been used widely as an alternative to chemical pesticides which, although cheap, can enter the food chain and can be rendered ineffective by the development of resistance. The recent observation of resistance to *B. thuringiensis* toxin due to over-application is a reminder that this phenomenon is not restricted to chemical agents. Proposed biocontrol agents, both bacteria and fungi, that colonise the rhizosphere and offer protection against plant pathogens are, at present, unmodified strains. This is also true of microorganisms and their products of potential use in the control of heavy metal pollution. Finally, it may inevitably become necessary in certain situations to use GMOs to bring about improvements in the environment. For some combinations of pollutants, especially chlorinated hydrocarbons, gene cloning will be required to extend the substrate range of microorganisms for release. The balancing of relative risks associated with the environmental impact of GMOs versus toxic chemicals will also apply in the paper industry where on-site, large-scale production of bleaching enzymes using a GMO will hopefully replace the use and subsequent discharge of chlorine.

3.6 Some case histories of deliberate release

(1) *Bacillus thuringiensis* strains produce a number of insecticidal crystal proteins (ICPs) that are toxic to a range of Lepidoptera, Diptera and Coleoptera, depending on the strain. The bacteria, and preparations of the ICPs, have been used to control agricultural pests for over 30 years. Recombinants with altered specificity have been generated both by "conventional" genetics and by genetic manipulation techniques. The genes have also been transferred to other plant-associated bacteria, including *Pseudomonas* and *Clavibacter*, with the aim of improving plant protection, and these have been released in field trials. The ICP genes have also been transferred (via *Agrobacterium*) to plants, conferring significant resistance to insect attack.

(2) Baculovirus is one of the best documented releases, not least for the exemplary manner in which the field trials were performed. Baculoviruses are widespread in the environment and infect insect larvae feeding on contaminated plant foliage. However, baculoviruses will only realise their full potential as pest control agents when genetic engineering enables improvement of their host range and virulence, and this is now within reach. Tests on genetically tagged strains provided valuable information on persistence and genetic stability so that the first physically uncontained field application was undertaken in 1989 with monitoring of engineered and natural virus populations continuing through 1992. The key to the smooth progress and development of these trials was the early demonstration that biological containment was effective in producing virus particles that were self-destructive and eliminated from the environment. The use of genetically engineered baculoviruses as agents for pest control has recently been reviewed exhaustively (Wood & Granados, 1991).

(3) Wild *Pseudomonas syringae* colonizes leaves and produces a protein that nucleates ice crystal formation, leading to crop damage. The GMO release was interesting for a number of reasons: the modified *P. syringae* strain did not contain additional DNA but had the gene for the ice nucleating protein deleted; it was an absolute requirement that the introduced strain outcompete and exclude the indigenous *P. syringae* from colonization of the leaf surface; it was the first release of live genetically modified bacteria approved by the U.S. Environmental Protection Agency and it attracted considerable public attention. The trial was a success in that the strawberry plants to which the ice-minus GMO was applied were not subsequently colonised by the indigenous *P. syringae*, a measure of frost protection was afforded to the treated plants and the recombinant bacteria did not become dispersed or established in the area surrounding the test plot.

(4) *Agrobacterium tumefaciens*, which causes crown gall tumours, has been successfully controlled in many plant nurseries by inoculation with a naturally-occurring nonpathogenic *Agrobacterium* strain that produces a toxin (agrocin) active only against other agrobacteria. Production of and resistance to this toxin is determined by plasmid-encoded genes,

and if conjugation in the field were to transfer the plasmid to pathogenic strains the inoculation programme might become ineffective. Recently, the toxin-producing plasmid has been modified to remove its transfer ability, and the resulting GMO has been approved for release in Australia. In this case, the GMO has no new genetic material, and it can be strongly argued that it is safer than the conventional strain that it replaces.

3.7 New approaches to the study of microbial communities

Concerns regarding the environmental impact of released GMOs quickly exposed the limitations of our understanding of microbial ecology. The requirement to be able to detect very low numbers of recombinant bacteria in natural environments was the first priority. Conventional dilution-plating techniques have limited sensitivity and only recover the viable, culturable fraction of the population. Some recent improvements have been made in extraction methodology and selective media, and direct detection by staining or the use of fluorescent antibodies linked to immunocapture methods. These approaches are all dependent on gene expression, but the real breakthroughs have been made in direct detection of nucleic acid sequences. Application of the **polymerase chain reaction** (PCR) has been central to the dramatic improvements in detection sensitivity and claims of the order of 1 cell detected per gram of sample in a background of 10^{10} diverse nontarget organisms are not uncommon (Steffan & Atlas, 1991). Of more fundamental interest is the potential of obtaining new insights into the diversity of microbial populations by direct analysis of the 16S ribosomal RNA sequences present. For several habitats, this approach has already revealed diversity far beyond that observed by isolating and identifying bacteria. The most difficult challenge for these new techniques will be the direct analysis of processes such as nitrification, where quantitative data could provide new information on the activity status and hence importance of species, including those that have not been cultured *in vitro*.

3.8 Summary

The complexity of microbial populations, and our understanding of them, is such that the risk of releasing genes into these populations cannot be defined and estimated precisely. Some released genes will undoubtedly survive and be transferred within bacterial communities, but horizontal gene transfers accompanied by mutations and genome rearrangements are a normal part of evolution. In fact, it is our ignorance of the genetics of bacterial populations in the environment that is a major hindrance to progress. There have perhaps been too many studies directed towards the tracking of plasmids and genes released into model systems containing populations that are poorly characterized. Direct analysis of nucleic acid and gene pools has now been facilitated by the development of convenient and rapid sequencing techniques, and this approach will define the diversity of the genetic background in which GMOs may find themselves.

4. RELEASE OF PLANTS

4.1 Application of genetic modification to plants
Genetic modification allows breeders to add genes (perhaps from entirely unrelated organisms) to the genome of a plant, which then confer useful (agricultural/horticultural) traits on the transgenic. As well as extending available genetic resources, these techniques can by-pass a number of conventional breeding problems, such as the need for lengthy backcrossing programmes.

Many characteristics that are controlled by single genes have already been introduced into a number of crop plants. Such traits include herbicide resistance, insect resistance, disease resistance, flower colour, metal and drought tolerance, and various nutritional and processing quality improvements. Plants that have been modified include many crops in western arable agriculture (apart from certain cereals), and several plants in other areas of agriculture such as market gardening, horticulture, soft fruits and forestry.

Multigenic traits, such as those involved with improved nutrient uptake, photosynthetic efficiency, nitrogen fixation and tolerance to a number of environmental stresses, require greater understanding of their genetics and biochemistry before improvements by genetic modification can be made.

In the future, the application of genetic modification to the production of industrial oils and chemicals, and to fine chemicals (secondary plant products and pharmaceuticals) is likely to be important. But for the present, many of the engineered traits are not novel to the plant breeder. Resistance to diseases and tolerance of herbicides, for example, have all been bred into crops by conventional crossing with wild relatives, without adverse effects. There has been considerable debate, however, about whether a genetically modified crop is more or less likely to produce unpredictable adverse effects than the same crop produced by conventional breeding techniques. The general consensus is that the method by which the modified plant is produced is of little consequence and that the product, not the process, should be regulated (NAS, 1987).

4.2 The perceived risks

Concerns about the risks of releasing genetically modified crop plants relate either to the expression of undesirable characteristics by the modified plant itself, or to negative effects following transfer of the gene to another crop or wild relative. Thus the three main concerns are as follows:

(1) the possibility of increased persistence as arable weeds

(2) the possibility of creating crops invasive of natural habitats

(3) the possibility of gene transfer to related crops or wild species, which then present ecological problems as persistent weeds or invaders of surrounding natural communities, with possible subsequent effects of the gene products on ecosystem structure and function.

4.3 Creating weedy or invasive crops

Most crops are highly selected for survival and reproduction under the restricted conditions of intense management. The probability of accidentally creating a weedy plant as a secondary effect of some other agriculturally useful trait introduced by genetic modification is, therefore, low. Various probabilities have been estimated for the chances of turning a crop into a weed. These range across several orders of magnitude, from 10^{-10} (Keeler, 1989) to 10^{-1} (Fitter *et al.*, 1990). The lower figure is based on the probability of altering a range of characters such as those listed by Baker (1965) (see Chapter 2) to turn a non-weed into a weed. However, Baker's traits have little predictive value in separating weedy from non-weedy members of closely related plant groups, and the higher figure is derived from a list of weedy crops. Many plants are weeds in one area but crops in other regions (Holm *et al.*, 1977) and require *no* change to become a weed although their degree of success is influenced by local environmental factors.

Can one, therefore, assess whether a genetically modified crop is likely to become a weed? It is possible that some traits might give a plant an advantage, allowing it to persist or spread. An increase in seed dormancy might enhance the persistence of plants in arable or natural habitats; but it is unlikely that this trait would be bred intentionally into crop plants, because farmers want their seed to germinate after sowing.

Herbicide tolerance could cause problems in agricultural systems that would require careful management, but it is unlikely to make crops more invasive of natural habitats where herbicides are not applied. The creation of invasive plants would involve alteration of the crop so that it was capable of population increase in surrounding natural habitats. Traits that might confer this include physiological tolerances that affect the range of conditions under which the plant can grow. Salt or drought tolerant plants, for example, might escape and colonize salt marshes or semi-arid lands. Theoretically, plants could become invasive when freed from pests and pathogens, although few plants other than introduced exotics appear to be kept scarce in natural communities by insect herbivores or diseases (Burdon, 1987; Crawley, 1989). It is important to consider all such characters, even though there would appear to be no suite of characters which reliably distinguish weeds from non-weeds (Perrins *et al.*, 1992).

The outcome of particular genetic changes cannot be predicted with certainty and will depend upon a combination of factors: the genetic construct, crop type, geographic location (*e.g.* the opportunity for outcrossing with weedy relatives and local crop genotypes, see below), and the ecosystem into which the crop is introduced. Information on these factors can be obtained from the published literature or from data bases (Brown & Crawley, 1991) and allows a preliminary assessment of risk and of the habitats in which the transgenic crop might be most invasive. Without direct experimental evidence, however, many of the risks are speculative.

In Britain, ecological risk assessment experiments are underway in natural habitats as part of the PROSAMO programme (Planned Release of Selected and Modified Organisms), in which the ecology of transgenic and non-transgenic crops is being compared in a range of different habitats and locations. The crops are sugar beet (*Beta vulgaris*), oilseed rape (*Brassica napus oleifera*), potato (*Solanum tuberosum*) and maize (*Zea mays*), with genes for herbicide resistance and kanamycin resistance as a marker. Factors affecting persistence and invasiveness such as the presence of herbivores, perennial plant competition and plant pathogens (Crawley, 1990), have been tested in various combinations, in replicate plots. Without cultivation and herbivore protection not a single seed sown reproduced (Cherfas 1990), and the data so far show no indication that the modified traits increase invasiveness or weediness of the crops investigated (Rees *et al.*, 1991).

4.4 Gene transfer
Gene transfer can occur through the production of a fertile hybrid between a genetically modified crop and a related crop or wild species. Backcrossing of the hybrid to one of the parents will spread the foreign gene by a process known as introgression. Whether or not hybrid weeds will become a problem in natural habitats will depend upon whether the transferred genes confer a fitness advantage, or at least confer no fitness disadvantage.

Assessment of the risk of gene transfer from a genetically modified crop to a related species needs to consider the various barriers to the production of fertile hybrids, such as the distance of pollen movement, flowering times and incompatibility barriers. Apart from the limits of pollen dispersal, these are relatively easy to measure or predict. Although most pollen is deposited within metres of the plant, pollen dispersal distances can vary enormously depending upon species and environmental conditions (Levin & Kerster, 1974). Indeed within continuous populations gene flow is generally restricted to a few metres, but between populations (Ellstrand, 1988) gene flow can be measured over distances of at least 1000m. Thus, the escape of modified genes into natural populations is possible for those crops that have local wild relatives. Some predictions can be made on the basis of the pollination mechanism of the plants involved, and several models for gene flow through pollen and the spread of hybrid organisms have been proposed (*e.g.* Manasse & Kareiva, 1991). Data needed to improve these risk assessment models can only be obtained by experimentation on a crop-by-crop basis.

Experiments to measure pollen transport, and to test the potential for hybridization of transgenic crops, are underway as part of the PROSAMO and other programmes (*e.g.* European Community Biotechnology Action Programme (BAP)). These include attempts to hybridize transgenic oil seed rape with various cruciferous weeds, and potato with wild solanaceous plants. Interspecific hybrids could only be achieved with difficulty, under forced conditions by embryo rescue, so the risk of hybridization of these crops in nature appears to be very low, regardless of the pattern of pollen movement. Fertile hybrids between a transgenic alfalfa (*Medicago sativa*) and several related species are more easily obtained (de Greef, 1990). Genetic transformation of perennial forage plants, such as alfalfa and pasture grasses, that are less highly selected for growth under intense management and are closer to wild types, may pose more of a threat of persistence or invasiveness.

If hybridization is a possibility, and gene transfer is of concern, then the modified crop should be grown as far away from related species as is practicable. Pollen movement could also be limited by growing male sterile crop plants or by surrounding the crop by guard rows to trap pollen.

4.5 British crops
Apart from pasture grasses, mentioned above, one of the very few examples from the British flora where there is evidence for hybridization between a crop and a wild species is sugar beet (*Beta vulgaris* ssp. *vulgaris*). This is a close relative of the wild sea beet (*Beta vulgaris* ssp. *maritima*) and there is circumstantial evidence for introgression between the two taxa based mainly on the occurrence of "bolters" (plants that flower in their first as opposed to second year of growth) amongst the beet crop. These are thought to be due to the introgression of "annual genes" from wild beets in southern Europe where most commercial sugar beet seed has been produced (Hornsey & Arnold, 1979). Prior to release of transgenic beet it will be necessary to investigate the incidence of hybridization between the crop and the British wild beets, and the relative performance of the transgenic and non-transgenic sugar beet in different environments.

Other issues that need to be examined include the incidence of feral crop populations and their mechanisms of establishment. For example, it is widely assumed that oilseed rape is becoming a weed in disturbed habitats such as roadsides. It is not known, however, whether the populations maintain themselves, or are replenished by seeds spilled during transport of the crop. This illustrates the need to examine the post-harvest processing of transgenic crops as well as their growth performance.

4.6 Summary

At present, the debate on environmental risks is largely conjectural because there is little direct evidence on the performance of modified crops in natural environments. Although most genetic modifications are not expected to cause adverse ecological effects, the present cautious case-by-case approach to risk assessment will build a body of evidence so that certain categories of crop and construct may be given generic permission for commercial introduction.

5.RELEASE OF ANIMALS

5.1 Introduction

To date, fewer animal species have been genetically modified than either plant or microbial species. However, the taxonomic range of GMOs produced includes nematodes, insects, sea urchins, fish, amphibians and mammals. Several species of large farm animals have been transformed but these are unlikely to be released or escape unnoticed and set up breeding populations in the wild. This chapter will, therefore, concentrate on some insects, using the genus *Drosophila* as an example, several fish species and small mammals, all of which are likely to breed if released, either accidentally or deliberately, into the environment. This will allow detailed consideration of the examples, while serving as a general illustration of the types of genetic modification attempted and the important issues involved. Unlike microorganisms and plants, there have been few documented releases of transgenic animals (Williamson *et al.*, 1990). This chapter will, therefore, examine the comparison frequently made between GMO release and the invasion of species and genotypes (Kapuscinski & Hallerman, 1990). A continuum of analogies can be made between introduced transgenic animals and introduced non-transgenic animals. Starting at the less worrying extreme, introduction of transgenic animals containing minor genetic alterations would be analogous to the introduction of rare or foreign non-transgenic genotypes. This would simply perturb single loci (see Fig. 5.1). At the other more worrying extreme, introduction of transgenic animals containing major genotype alterations, may be more analogous to the introduction of closely related, non-native species.

5.2 Types of genetic modification

As an example of why biologists may wish to release animals into the environment for scientific purposes, we can look at *Drosophila melanogaster* and heat shock proteins (hsps). These are known to be produced when cells are exposed to extraneous stresses such as heat or poisons. Research carried out at University College, London, was aimed at investigating the temperature microclimate experienced by individual flies in the wild. The idea was to measure directly the effect of temperature on the production of hsps. However, measuring protein levels directly in a large number of flies, captured from the wild, is difficult. Transgenic flies were, therefore, constructed with the hsp promoter directing the synthesis of alcohol dehydrogenase (ADH), a readily assayed enzyme. In this way, the temperature experienced by the flies at any one time could have been estimated from the level of ADH activity. Such experiments, using molecular markers to measure environmental variables experienced by insects, may in the future become a major source of release requests.

To illustrate how transgenic animals might come to enter the environment accidentally, we can look at two examples from vertebrates. Zhang *et al.* (1990) showed that common carp (*Cyprinus carpio*) which were transgenic for a rainbow trout growth hormone gene with a **constitutive promoter** were significantly larger than non-transgenic siblings. Such fish would be of obvious interest to aquaculture. Other species of fish are also the subject of applied transgenic research. Aquaculture involves contained environments (tanks, ponds, cages, etc.) but accidental escapes are possible. Many genes have now been introduced into mice, in connection with studies of gene expression and embryonic development. For example one study, using a mouse immunoglobulin kappa gene (Storb *et al.*, 1984), was aimed at revealing the mechanisms of tissue-specific gene expression. It was possible to show that the expression of the intact introduced gene, at the new chromosomal locus, was still tissue specific (B lymphocytes). Once again, while animal house containment procedures are rigorous, accidental escapes are always possible. However, most strains of laboratory mice and rats are highly inbred or otherwise less fit than wild genotypes.

5.3 Ecological risks: the species invasion model

As discussed in Chapter 2, introductions of exotic species are frequently successful (*i.e.* they become established) (perhaps 10%) and sometimes produce environmental problems (perhaps 1%), such as explosive population increase or loss of native species diversity. A number of *Drosophila* species have successfully invaded new areas. Of particular interest is *Drosophila subobscura*, a widespread and common European species, that has successfully invaded into both North (Beckenbach & Prevosti,1986), and South America (Brncic & Budnik, 1987). In Chile,

D. subobscura was first detected in 1978, in an area routinely sampled for drosophilids since 1954. By 1979, it comprised 50% of the *Drosophila* fauna in this region and has spread to include a region from 29º-53º S (Brncic & Budnik, 1987). Coincident with this invasion, one of the endemic species, *D. pavani*, which before 1979 consistently comprised 40%-60% of the *Drosophila* fauna, has become quite rare (1%-4%).

Data compiled by Welcomme (1988) from 1354 introductions of 237 species of fish into 140 countries showed that nearly 60% of introductions became established. More importantly, 23.7% of introductions became a significant or dominant element of the host fauna with 89 cases (6.6%) having sufficient impact on the local environment or fish stocks to cause serious concern. Why these figures are higher for fish (cf. Chapter 2) is not clear.

Eight species of small mammal have been introduced to the British Isles, including the house mouse (*Mus musculus*), the wild ancestor of the laboratory mouse. The house mouse probably originated in Central Asia from where it has spread world-wide. However, it lives mainly as a commensal with humans, and only occasionally invades natural habitats. Exceptions to this are Australian heathland and sclerophyll forest, and Californian coastal sage. Even so, studies suggest that it is out-competed by native species (Lidicker, 1966; Fox & Pople, 1984) and there is no evidence of serious impact upon native habitats.

An interesting speculation about 'animal invasions' is mentioned by Crawley (1986). A resilient idea in ecology is that carnivores are resource (competition) limited while herbivores are predator limited. If competition is an important determinant of community structure, then carnivores should find it more difficult to invade than herbivores. Crawley examined invasions in British birds and mammals and found significantly more herbivores than carnivores among the invaders when compared to the abundance of these groups in the native fauna.

5.4 Ecological risks: the genotype invasion model
There are few examples of well documented genotype invasion in the literature. Two examples with *Drosophila* species are perhaps

exceptional. Australian workers (Barker & East, 1980; Barker *et al.*, 1989) released genotypes of *D. buzzatii*, which feeds upon rot pockets in *Opuntia stricta*, into two isolated wild populations. The loci perturbed were esterase-2, ß-N-acetylhexosaminase and alcohol dehydrogenase. Figure 5.1 shows the results for the ADH allele. In a set of earlier experiments (Dobzhansky & Wright, 1943, 1947), American workers had released individuals of *D. pseudoobscura* containing the third chromosome recessive marker called *orange*. In both sets of experiments, the invading genotype was maintained in the wild population initially by migration (release) but rapidly removed after release had stopped. No effect on the invaded community of *Drosophila* species was noticed. However, this was not carefully monitored since it was not the primary objective of these experiment.

There have been many examples of introductions of conspecific stocks of fish into natural environments, generally with the aim of 'improving' or supplementing the existing stocks for exploitation. While some documented cases using genetic markers (Altukhov & Salmenkova, 1987; Pastene *et al.*, 1991) show little effect of the introductions on the native stocks in salmonid species (the best studied group), the growing appreciation of interpopulation genetic variation and its possible adaptive value (Stahl, 1987; Ferguson, 1989) has led to a conservative attitude towards introductions among most fisheries scientists. It is generally recommended that where restocking takes place, the hatchery should use wild-caught broodstock and endeavour to have minimal genetic impact on wild stocks (Ryman, 1991).

5.5 Ecological risks: contained experiments

An alternative to using comparisons with species invasion or genotype invasion is to use contained experimental releases. This has been done for both drosophilid flies and for fishes.

Transgenic *Drosophila melanogaster*, containing two foreign genes, have been released into large cages designed to be a microcosm of the flies natural environment (Shorrocks *et al.*, 1993). The cages contained over 1000 grapes as a resource, a portion of which were renewed weekly. The two genes were neomycin phosphotransferase II (NPTII), used as a

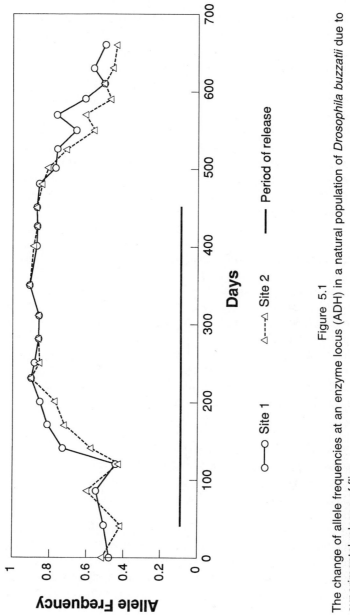

Figure 5.1

The change of allele frequencies at an enzyme locus (ADH) in a natural population of *Drosophila buzzatii* due to experimental release of flies.

selectable marker for identifying transformed individuals, and bacterial ß-galactosidase, under the control of a composite *Drosophila* Hsp27-*hairy* promoter. After approximately 20 generations, changes in frequency of the two genes suggested that selection was density-dependent, with the foreign genes increasing at low densities (below 27 females per grape). Since natural densities are below this value, these experiments suggest that if released these two genes would spread.

Transgenic common carp (see 5.1) are currently the subject of trials in contained outdoor ponds in the USA. In assessing new genetically modified fish, tests could move from lowest risk environments (indoor research laboratories) to less contained environments as more information for risk assessment becomes known. This is further discussed by Kapuscinski & Hallerman (1990). Techniques for suppression of reproduction are also available to reduce the risk of establishment of accidental or deliberate introductions of fish. Monosex stocks can be produced in several species of commercial interest and **triploidy** can be induced which effectively sterilises females (some male triploids can produce **aneuploid** sperm). A combination of the two techniques (all-female triploids) may be the safest measure.

5.6 Horizontal transfer and introgression
The invasion of **P-elements** into *D. melanogaster* is a relatively recent event. Only strains isolated from the wild prior to about 1950, and subsequently maintained in the laboratory, lack P-elements. Worldwide surveys of wild populations at the present time have failed to reveal any populations of this species that do not contain P-elements. Several lines of evidence suggest that P-elements were transferred horizontally into *D. melanogaster* from a distantly related species, *D. willistoni*, prior to 1950. Evidence for this event includes: (a) the near identity of P-element sequences from *D. melanogaster* and *D. willistoni*; (b) the high sequence conservation between all P-elements in *D. melanogaster*; (c) the lack of P-elements in other members of the *melanogaster* species group compared to their widespread occurrence in members of the willistoni group; (d) range overlap of the two species in Florida and Central and South America; (e) a likely vector in the form of a mite, *Proctolaelaps regalis* (Houck *et al.,* 1991).

Introgression of genes from one species of fish into another where fertile hybrids are produced (*e.g.* tilapias: see Pullin, 1988) has been observed, often as a result of species transfers by man. Engineered genes could also be transmitted in the case of such species combinations.

There is no evidence for introgression of genes from one species of small mammal into another. However, there is evidence of invasion of *Felis catus* genes into the Scottish wild cat (*F. sylvestris grampia*) and the African wild cat (*F. lybica*) through hybridization (Drake *et al.*, 1989).

5.7 Summary

The present rather tentative position is, therefore, that invasion of exotic species is frequently successful and may be damaging while the invasion of exotic genotypes (within native species) is less so. Since most future releases will likely involve genetically modified native species, the genotype model is likely to be the one most suitable for predicting the effects of GMO release. The release of transgenic exotic species, or those involving major genotypic modification may result in the kind of environmental disturbance associated with the invasion of exotic species. However, there are no experimental data on species invasion and there are no comparative assessments of the two extreme models (species *versus* genotypes) using the same species and the same environments. This is an urgent priority.

6. DISCUSSION

Any new procedure, especially involving manipulation of the environment, is subject to a certain amount of risk. The question is whether the risk is large or small, and whether the potential benefits (which may also be environmental) outweigh the possible costs. As in other areas of human endeavour, genetic manipulation both promises to save the world we have, and threatens to destroy the world as we know it. How real is this risk?

Because of our present ignorance of the reasons why some species or genotypes invade, and others do not, in the majority of cases risk assessment will be more art than science, and will rely heavily on informed opinion. There will clearly be genetic constructs that are unsuitable for release, and so care must be taken to assess the potential risks of release on a case-by-case basis. The problems that will need to be addressed will be different in microbes, plants and animals.

We have argued that, in many cases, GMOs differ only in detail from their natural progenitors. All organisms use the same genetic system. Genetic manipulation has given us the ability to move functional genes both within and between species, using methods adapted from, but not new to natural processes. The introduced DNA sequences generally behave in exactly the same manner as the normal genes within the host organism. Gene transfer and genetic rearrangements are natural processes that underpin biological evolution and are ongoing within species.

For deliberate release experiments, it is the phenotype of the organism that matters, not how it was made. In this context, ecologists can make very significant contributions to predicting the behaviour of transgenics in the environment by studying similar, naturally-occurring phenotypes. The examples we have of invasion are of the accidental or deliberate release of exotic species. Although these examples may provide some insight into the possible fate of released GMOs, the more appropriate model is the release of novel genotypes of a native species, an area of research about which little is known. It must be stressed that problems arising from the introduction of organisms which are both exotic and transgenic may be largely the result of the exotic rather than transgenic nature of the organism. Since most future releases will probably involve genetically modified native species, the genotype model is likely to be the one most suitable for predicting the effects of GMO release. However, there is a lack of experimental work on species invasion, and the lack of comparative assessments of the two extreme models (species *versus* genotypes) using the same species and the same environments limits our ability to produce predictions. This is an urgent priority for future research.

The release of transgenic foreign species, or those involving major genotypic transformation may result in the kind of environmental disturbance associated with the invasion of exotic species. Although the vast majority of genetic modifications are not expected to cause adverse ecological effects, the present cautious, case-by-case approach to risk assessment will build a body of evidence such that certain categories of organism and construct may be given generic permission for commercial or experimental introduction. In all cases, assessments of the likely impact of the modified organisms, and suitable control measures where little is known, are essential to the continued safe use of genetically modified organisms.

7. REFERENCES

Altukhov, Y.P. & Salmenkova, E.A. (1987). Stock transfer relative to natural organisation, management, and conservation of fish populations. In: *Population genetics and fisheries management.* (Eds. Ryman, N. & Utter, F.), pp. 333-343, University of Washington Press, Seattle.

Baker, H.G. (1965). Characteristics and modes of origin of weeds. In: *Genetics of Colonizing Species.* (Eds. Baker, H.G. & Stebbins, G.L.). Academic Press Inc., New York.

Barker, J.S.F. & East, P.D. (1980). Evidence for selection following perturbation of allozyme frequencies in a natural population of *Drosophila. Nature,* **284,** 166-168.

Barker, J.S.F., East, P.D. & Christiansen, F. (1989). Estimation of migration from a perturbation experiment in natural populations of *Drosophila buzzatii* Paterson & Wheeler. *Biological Journal of the Linnean Society,* **37,** 311-334.

Beckenbach, A.T. & Prevosti, A. (1986). Colonization of North America by the European species, *Drosophila subobscura* and *D. ambigua. American Midland Naturalist,* **115,** 10-18.

Brncic, D. & Budnik, M. (1987). Some interactions of the colonizing species *Drosophila subobscura* with local *Drosophila* in Chile. *Genetica Iberica,* **39,** 249-267.

Brown, S.L. & Crawley, M.J. (1991). *Environmental Risk Assessment Considerations for Certain Genetically Modified Plants.* Report for the European Commission, Contract reference B6614/90/011521.

Burdon, J.J. (1987). *Diseases and Plant Population Biology.* Cambridge University Press, Cambridge.

Cherfas, J. (1990). Transgenic crops get a test in the wild. *Science,* **251,** 878.

Crawley, M.J. (1986). The population biology of invaders. *Philosophical Transactions of the Royal Society of London B,* **314:** 711-731.

Crawley, M.J. (1987). What makes a community invasible? In: *Colonization, Succession and Stability.* (Eds. Gray, A.J. Crawley, M.J. & Edwards, P.J.). Blackwell Scientific Publications, Oxford.

Crawley, M.J. (1989). The relative importance of vertebrate and invertebrate herbivores in plant population dynamics. In: *Insect-Plant Interactions* 1.(Ed. Bernays, E.A.), pp.45-71. CRC Press, Boca Raton, Florida.

Crawley, M.J. (1990). The ecology of genetically engineered organisms: assessing the environmental risks. In: *Introduction of Genetically Modified Organisms into the Environment.* (Eds. Mooney, H.A. & Bernardi, G.), pp.133-150. Scientific Committee on Problems of the Environment (SCOPE) **44**. John Wiley and Sons, Chichester.

De Greef, W. (1990). The release of transgenic plants into the environment. In: *Biotechnology R&D in the EC,* Part **1**. (Ed. Economidis, I.), pp.19-22. Commission of the European Communities.

Dobzhansky, T. & Wright, S. (1943). The genetics of natural populations X. Dispersion rates in *Drosophila pseudoobscura. Genetics*, **28**, 304-340.

Dobzhansky, T. & Wright, S. (1943). The genetics of natural populations XV. Rate of diffusion of a mutant gene through a population of *Drosophila pseudoobscura. Genetics*, **32**, 303-324.

Drake, J.A., Mooney, H.A., di Castri, F., Groves, R.H., Kruger, F.J., Rejmanek, M. & Williamson, M.H. (eds) (1989). *Biological Invasions: a Global Perspective.* Wiley, Chichester. 525 pp.

Ebenhard, T. (1988). Introduced birds and mammals and their ecological effects. *Swedish Wildlife Research (Viltrevy)*, **13(4)**, 5-107.

Elton, C. (1958). *The Ecology of Invasions by Animals and Plants.* Methuen, London. 181 pp.

Ferguson, A. (1989). Genetic differences among brown trout, *Salmo trutta*, stocks and their importance for the conservation and management of the species. *Freshwater Biology*, **21**, 35-46.

Fitter, A., Perrins, J. & Williamson, M. (1990). Weed probability challenged. *BioTechnology*, **8**, 473.

Fox, B.J. & Pople, R. (1984). Experimental confirmation of interspecific competition between native and introduced mice. *Australian Journal of Ecology*, **9**, 323-334.

Fry, J.C. & Day, M.J.(eds.) (1990). *Bacterial Genetics in Natural Environments.* Chapman and Hall, London. 259pp.

Gray, A.J. (1986). Do invading species have definable genetic characteristics? *Philosophical Transactions of the Royal Society of London B*, **314**, 655-674.

Gray, A.J., Marshall, D.F. & Raybold, A.F. (1991). A century of evolution in *Spartina anglica. Advances in Ecological Research*, **21**, 1-62.

Groves (1986). Plant invasions of Australia: an overview. In: *Ecology of Biological Invasions* (Eds. Groves, R.H. & Burdon, J.J.). Cambridge University Press, Cambridge.

Herbold, B. & Moyle, P.B. (1986). Introduced species and vacant niches *American Naturalist*, **128** , 751-760.

Hirsch, P.R. & Spokes, J.R. (1988). *Rhizobium leguminosarum* as a model for investigating gene transfer in soil. In: *Risk Assessment for Deliberate Releases.* (Ed. Klingmuller, W.), pp.10-17. Springer-Verlag, Berlin.

Holm, L.G., Plucknett, D.L., Pancho, J.V. & Herberger, J.P. (1977). *The World's Worst Weeds.* University Press, Honolulu.

Hornsey, K.G. & Arnold, M.H. (1979). The origins of weed beet. *Annals of Applied Biology*, **92**, 279-285.

Houck, M.A., Clark, J.B., Peterson, K.R. & Kidwell, M.G. (1991). Possible horizontal transfer of *Drosophila* genes by the mite *Proctolaelaps regalis*. *Science*, **253**, 1125-1129.

Kapuscinski, A.R. & Hallerman, E.M. (1990). Transgenic fish and public policy: anticipating environmental impacts of transgenic fish. *Fisheries*, **15**, 2-11.

Keeler, K.H. (1989). Can genetically engineered crops become weeds? *BioTechnology*, **1**, 1134-1139.

Lawton, J.H. & Brown, K.C. (1986). The population and community ecology of invading insects. *Philosophical Transactions of the Royal Society of London B*, **314** , 607-617.

Levin, S.A. (1989). Analysis of risk for invasions and control programs. In: *Biological Invasions: A Global Perspective.* (Ed. Drake, J. *et al.*) John Wiley and Sons Ltd., Chichester.

Levin, S.A. (1990). Ecological issues related to the release of genetically modified organisms into the environment. In: *Introduction of Genetically Modified Organisms into the Environment.* (Eds. Mooney, H.A. & Bernadi, G.) John Wiley and Sons Ltd., Chichester.

Levin, D.A. & Kerster, H.W. (1974). Gene flow in seed plants. *Evolutionary Biology*, **7**, 139-220.

Lidicker, W.Z. (1966). Ecological observations on a feral house mouse population declining to extinction. *Ecological Monographs*, **36**, 27-50.

Manasse, R. & Karieva, P. (1991). Quantifying the spread of recombinant genes and organisms. In: *Assessing Ecological Risks of Biotechnology.* (Ed. Ginzburg, L.R.), pp.215-231. Butterworth-Heinemann, Boston.

Murrell, J.C. & Roberts L.M. (1989). *Understanding Genetic Engineering.* John Wiley and Sons, New York. 132 pp.

NAS (1987). *Introduction of Recombinant DNA-Engineered Organisms into the Environment: Key Issues.* National Academy Press, Washington, D.C.

Newsome, A.E. & Noble, I.R. (1986). Ecological and physiological characters of invading species. In: *Ecology of Biological Invasions.* (Eds. Groves, R.H. & Burdon, J.J.), pp. 1-20. Cambridge University Press, Cambridge.

Old, R.W. & Primrose, S.B. (1989). *Principles of Gene Manipulation.* 4th Edn. Blackwell Scientific Publications, Oxford. 438 pp.

Pastene, L.A., Numachi, K. & Tsukamoto, K. (1991). Examination of reproductive success of transplanted stocks in an amphidromous fish, *Plecoglossus altivelis* (Temmink et Schlegel) using mitochondrial DNA and isozyme markers. *Journal of Fish Biology*, **39** (Suppl. A), 93-100.

Perrins, J., Williamson, M., & Fitter, A. (1992). A survey of differing views of weed classification: implications for regulation of introductions. *Biological Conservation*, **60**, 47-56.

Prince, R.C. (1992). Bioremediation of oil spills, with particular reference to the spill from the Exxon Valdez. In: *Microbial Control of Pollution.* (Eds. Fry, J.C. *et al.*), pp.19-34. Cambridge University Press, Cambridge.

Pullin, R.S.V. (1988). *Tilapia Genetic Resources for Aquaculture.* ICLARM, Manila. 108pp.

Rees, M., Kohn, D., Hails, R., Crawley, M. & Malcolm, S. (1991). An ecological perspective to risk assessment. In: *Biological Monitoring of Genetically Engineered Plants and Microbes.* (Eds. MacKenzie, D.R. & Henry, S.C.), pp. 9-24. Proceedings of the Kiawah Island Conference, Nov 1990. Agricultural Research Institute, Bethesda, Maryland.

Royal Commission (1989). *13th Report on Environmental Pollution.* HMSO. 144pp.

Ryman, N. (1991). Conservation genetics considerations in fishery management. *Journal of Fish Biology*, **39** (Suppl. A), 211-224.

Shorrocks, B., Coates, D., Dytham, C., O'Brien, L., Berthier, E. & Dooher, K. (1992). Selection in favour of transgenic *Drosophila* in a 'released' population. Department of the Environment Report.

Simberloff, D. (1981). Community effects of introduced species. In: *Biotic Crises in Ecological and Evolutionary Time.* (Ed. Nitecki, M.H.), pp.53-81. Academic Press, New York.

Simberloff, D. (1991). Keystone species and community effects of biological introductions. In: *Assessing the Risks of Biotechnology* (Ed. Ginzberg, L.R.), pp.1-19. Butterworth-Heinemann, Boston.

Stahl, G. (1987). Genetic population structure of Atlantic salmon. In: *Population genetics and fisheries management.* (Eds. Ryman, N. & Utter, F.), pp. 121-140. University of Washington Press, Seattle.

Steffan, R.J. & Atlas, R.M. (1991). Polymerase chain reaction: applications in environmental microbiology. *Annual Review of Microbiology*, **45**, 69-87.

Storb, U., O'Bried, R., McMullen, M., Gollahon, K. & Brinster, R.L. (1984). High expression of cloned immunoglobulin kappa gene in transgenic mice is restricted to B lymphocytes. *Nature*, **310**, 238-241.

Stotzky, G. & Babich, H. (1986). Survival of, and genetic transfer by, genetically engineered bacteria in natural environments. *Advances in Applied Microbiology*, **31**, 93-138.

Welcomme, R.L. (compiler) (1988). International introductions of inland aquatic species. *FAO Fish Technology Papers*, **294**, 318pp.

Williamson, M.H. (1993). Invaders, weeds and the risks from GMO's. *Experimentia* (in press).

Williamson, M.H. & Brown, K.C. (1986). The analysis and modelling of British invasions. *Philosophical Transactions of the Royal Society of London B*, **314**, 505-522.

Williamson, M.H., Perrins, J. & Fitter, A. (1990). Releasing genetically engineered plants: present proposals and possible hazards. *Trends in Ecology and Evolution*, **5**, 417-419.

Wood, H.A. & Granados, R.R. (1991). Genetically engineered baculoviruses as agents for pest control. *Annual Reviews of Microbiology*, **45**, 69-87.

Young, J.P.W. & Wexler, M. (1988). Sym plasmid and chromosomal genotypes are correlated in field populations of *Rhizobium leguminosarum. Journal of General Microbiology* , **134** , 2731-2739.

Zhang, P., Hayat, M., Joyce, C., Gonzalez-Villasenor, L.I., Lin, C.M., Dunham, R.A., Chen, T.T. & Powers, D.A. (1990). Gene transfer, expression and inheritance of pRSV-rainbow trout-GH cDNA in the common carp, *Cyprinus carpio* (L.). *Molecular and Reproductive Development*, **25**, 3-13.

8. GLOSSARY

Amplification. Increasing the number of copies of a region of DNA, either by cloning into a vector or by using PCR.

Aneuploid. An organism bearing an irregular number of chromosomes. For example, if the diploid chromosome number is 2n, then one type of aneuploid would be 2n+1.

cDNA (complementary DNA). The DNA complement of an RNA sequence synthesised by the enzyme reverse transcriptase. The single- stranded DNA product can be made double-stranded using the enzyme DNA polymerase.

Chromatin. The DNA-protein complex used by the cell to package the genetic material in the nucleus and chromosomes.

Cloning vector. A DNA molecule, usually a plasmid or bacteriophage, into which foreign DNA fragments may be inserted (cloned).

Coding region. A DNA sequence made up of base triplets corresponding to the coded amino acids in the protein product.

Conjugation. The transfer of DNA from one bacterial cell to another.

Constitutive promoter. A promoter that is active in all cell types and at all stages of development.

DNA cloning. The insertion of a gene or DNA sequence into a vector molecule. This recombinant molecule is then transferred into a suitable host, *e.g. E. coli*, and the colony (clone) that results consists of cells that all contain the recombinant DNA molecule.

DNA library. A mixture of vector molecules each containing different fragments of genomic or complementary DNA.

Enhancer sequences. A sequence of DNA bases that can increase transcription from a gene even when located up to several kilobases away.

Eukaryotes. Organisms which have their genome divided into a number of chromosomes contained within a nucleus (e.g. plants, animals and fungi).

Exotic species. A species not indigenous to the native fauna or flora. The term encompasses both natural invaders and those introduced by humans, such as new agricultural species. The terms foreign and alien are also used.

P-elements. A family of transposable elements found in some *Drosophila* species.

Plasmid. An extrachromosomal circular DNA molecule capable of autonomous replication.

Polymerase chain reaction (PCR). This is a method of amplifying specific, short regions of DNA, using a heat stable DNA polymerase. Once many copies of a DNA sequence of interest are produced, it can be examined using other techniques such as electrophoresis.

Prokaryotes. Organisms in which the genome consists of a single circular DNA molecule residing in the cytoplasm of the cell (*i.e.* bacteria).

Promoter. The sequence of bases in a DNA molecule that enables RNA polymerase to recognise where genes begin.

Recombinant DNA. A DNA molecule containing a new combination of base sequences that have been spliced together *in vitro* using recombinant DNA technology.

Regulatory region. A DNA sequence involved in regulating the expression of genes (*e.g.* promoters).

Restriction enzyme. Enzymes which recognize and catalyse cleavage of double-stranded DNA sequences at specific sites on each strand.

Transcription. The process in which a single-stranded RNA molecule (mRNA), complementary to a DNA template, is synthesised by RNA polymerase.

Transduction. The transfer of bacterial genes from one bacterium to another by a bacteriophage particle.

Transformation. The introduction of exogenous DNA into cells.

Transgenic. An organism in which a foreign DNA sequences (from the same or a different species) is found within the genome of nearly every cell.

Translation. The synthesis of a polypeptide, using messenger RNA as a template.

Transposable element. A transposable element is a piece of DNA that can move around within and between genomes.

Triploid. An organism containing three sets of the basic number of chromosomes. If haploid = n (the basic number) and diploid = 2n (most animals and higher plants), then triploid = 3n.

9. LIST OF CONTRIBUTORS

Sue Brown — *Department of Biology, Imperial College at Silwood Park, Ascot S15 7PY.*

David Coates — *Department of Pure and Applied Biology, University of Leeds, Leeds LS2 9JT.*

Calvin Dytham — *Department of Biology, University of York, York YO1 5DD.*

Alan McCarthy — *Department of Genetics and Microbiology, University of Liverpool, PO Box 147, Liverpool L69 3BX.*

David Penman — *Institute of Aquaculture, University of Stirling, Stirling FK9 4LA.*

Alan Raybould — *Institute of Terrestrial Ecology, Furzebrook Research Station, Wareham BH20 5AS.*

Bryan Shorrocks — *Department of Pure and Applied Biology, University of Leeds, Leeds LS2 9JT.*

Andrew Watkinson — *Department of Biological Sciences, University of East Anglia, Norwich NR4 7TJ.*

Peter Young — *Department of Biology, University of York, York YO1 5DD.*